ESTHER

God Unseen

CHRISTI ROBILLARD

To my brother, Kirk:

Peace, be still. Lay all your worries down. Be still, oh my soul.
For our God, is in control. And if God is for us,
Then whom shall I fear? And our God is for us,
So lay down, be still.
He is God.
Hallelujah, our God has overcome.
Hallelujah, our Lord, Jesus Christ has won!

Lyrics by Sherri Youngward ©1999

CONTENTS

Prelude

It's the end of a long day and all you want to do is go home and put your feet up! As you are driving home your thoughts wander a bit as you reflect on your day; especially things you could have done differently and probably will do differently tomorrow, given the opportunity. You are in no mood for thoughtless drivers, you're on a mission—"get home!" As you approach an intersection the signal light just turns yellow, your typical modus operandi is to accelerate through the intersection before the light turn's red! But for some reason, even though you have plenty of time to safely drive through the intersection—you decide to break, coming to a firm stop. Within fractions of a second, two cars, side by side, barrel through the intersection at high speed; an apparent street race between two young drivers! Whew, that was close!

What are your immediate thoughts? Is it a coincidence that you decide to stop at the yellow signal light instead of racing through? Or, is it something more? Is it God? Is God directing your thoughts in imperceptible ways that cause you to make a decision to stop when you can normally drive safely through the intersection?

We all have distinct experiences when we can without a doubt say, "That was God!" But for most of our days, we traverse being clueless at how detailed God really is involved in our daily existence. He is in our thoughts, our activities and interactions; our past, our present and our future. He is in the best of days and in the worst of days. When we see Him and when we don't see Him. God is often *unseen* in the details of our daily lives—but He is there!

"It is good when He sends the visible evidence, but we appreciate it even more after we have trusted God without it. And those who are the most inclined to trust God without any evidence except His Word always receive the greatest amount of visible evidence of His love."
–*Charles Gallaudet Trumbull*

It is the conviction of most Christians that God is active in every aspect of their lives; and that He is an involved loving Heavenly Father who has good plans for His children. And so, we thank Him for His daily care, provision and protection—even when we are not aware of every detail of His involvement!

The story of Esther epitomizes *God Unseen.* He is present and active in the apparent coincidences of daily life . . . He is in the desires of a king and servants; and in the folly and wisdom of men. *God is all in all,* and *He does all things well!*

Introduction

ESTHER: GOD UNSEEN is a Bible study which is formatted as a five week course. Each lesson contains curriculum for two chapters of Esther. This Bible study is designed for *examination of pertinent points* of the text, *optimum group discussion,* and encouragement towards *spiritual renewal.* There is an important timely message to the Church in the book of Esther! It is the prayer of the writer that God will use these lessons to renew: faith, hope, intimacy, passion, and holiness. It is best to read all of Esther in one sitting to acquaint yourself with the story before beginning the lessons. Pray for *ears to hear what the Spirit is saying* . . . and look for *God Unseen!*

THE TIMES

The story of Esther historically fits between chapters 6 and 7 of Ezra; between the first return to Jerusalem led by Zerubbabel, and the second return led by Ezra. It provides the only biblical portrait of the vast majority of Jews who choose to remain in Persia rather than return to Jerusalem after the Babylonian captivity.

The Jews become comfortable while in captivity. They build homes, have families, and businesses. When the opportunity arises for the Jews to leave and return to their homeland, most choose to remain in voluntary exile.

Ahasuerus is king of Persia and reigns from India to Ethiopia, which includes over 127 provinces, during 486—464 B.C.

THE CENTRAL CHARACTERS

Ahasuerus, is the king's title in Hebrew. It means "high father" or "venerable king." It is used in the same way "Caesar" is as a title but does not identify the man. His Persian name is Khshayarshan, and Xerxes is his Greek name. He is the son of Darius 1, and inherits his kingdom from his father. His grandfather is Cyrus the Great. Ahasuerus rules over the Persian Empire from 486—464 B.C. He is a prideful, blundering man; a buffoon, unsettled in all his ways, which makes him a very dangerous king. *Vashti,* is the beautiful queen of Persia married to Ahasuerus. She is deposed of her position in marriage and in the kingdom because she chooses to challenge the king's authority by disobeying his request. *Haman,* the Agagite, is a descendent from king Agag. His family associations place him among a people that are Israel's enemies. He is the villain of the story and his hateful heart is exposed for full viewing. *Mordecai,* is the Jewish cousin of Esther who becomes her father-figure and guardian. His humble origins are only emphasized by his rise in position and power. He is a man governed by integrity, honor, and wisdom. *Esther,* derived from the Persian word "Star," is a Jew. Her Hebrew name is Hadassah, "Myrtle." Interestingly, the Latin title for this book is Hester, meaning "hidden." Esther is orphaned as a young girl and lives in the capital city, Susa, or Shushan, in Hebrew, with her cousin, Mordecai. Esther is well known for her beauty.

THE SUMMARY

The book of Esther never mentions: heaven, hell, worship, prayer or the Hebrew law. God's name is never mentioned in the book of Esther—but God is there! We hear Him. See Him. Feel Him! We are always aware of His presence as we navigate through the events of this story. His provision and protection are clearly seen, along with several allusions to His direct involvement. Esther and the Song of Solomon are the only two books in the Bible which do not mention God by name.

The book of Esther is written to show how the Jewish people are protected and preserved by the gracious hand of God from the threat of annihilation. Although God disciplines His covenant people, He never abandons them. The God of Israel is the sovereign controller of history, and His providential care and heartbeat can be seen throughout this book.

Although a decree is signed for annihilation of the Jews, a second decree allows them to overthrow their enemies. Being fewer in number than their enemies—amazingly, they become greater in power, overthrowing them! Evidence of *God Unseen* is unmistakable!

The Jews defeat their enemies in the cities throughout the Persian provinces, but do not take the plunder. The next day becomes a day of celebration and an annual Jewish holiday called the Feast of Purim. The word is derived from the Assyrian *puru,* meaning "lot," referring to the lots cast by Haman to determine the day decreed for the Jewish annihilation.

"Now faith is the substance of things hoped for, the evidence of things not seen."
Hebrews 11:1

People, plans, power and privilege, all converge to accomplish the providence of God in the book of Esther; and that's a powerful and timely message to the Church! We live in a rapidly changing world—threats from all sides. But God remains *the same yesterday, today, and forever!* God is faithful, and God will fulfill all of His good promises!

PERSIAN EMPIRE TIME OF ESTHER

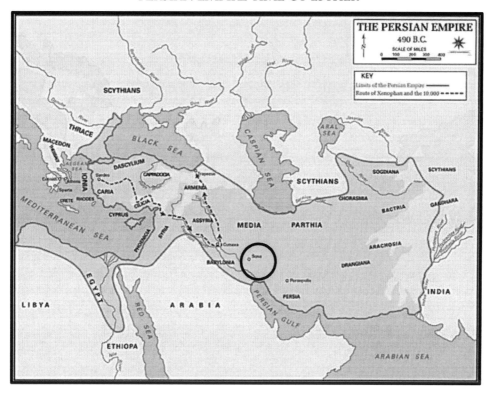

PRESENT DAY

TIMELINE

	THREAT TO THE JEWS		TRIUMPH OF THE JEWS	
REFERENCE	1:1————————2:21————————5:1		————————8:4————————————10:3	
DIVISION	SELECTION OF QUEEN ESTHER	FORMULATION OF PLOT BY HAMAN	TRIUMPH OF MORDECAI OVER HAMAN	TRIUMPH OF ISRAEL OVER ENEMIES
TOPIC	FEASTS OF AHASUERUS		FEASTS OF ESTHER AND PURIM	
	GRAVE DANGER		GREAT DELIVERANCE	
LOCATION	P E R S I A			
TIME	10 YEARS 483—473 B.C.			

THE JEWISH CALENDAR

MONTHS	CORRESPONDS WITH	NO. OF DAYS	MONTH OF CIVIL YEAR	MONTH OF SACRED YEAR
TISHRI	SEPT. – OCT.	30 days	1st	7th
HESHVAN	OCT. – NOV.	20 or 30 days	2nd	8th
CHISLEV	NOV. – DEC.	29 or 30 days	3rd	9th
TEBETH	DEC. – JAN.	29 days	4th	10th
SHEBAT	JAN. – FEB.	30 days	5th	11th
ADAR	FEB. – MAR.	29 or 30	6th	12th
NISAN	MAR. – APR.	30 days	7th	1st
IYAR	APR. – MAY	29 days	8th	2nd
SIVAN	MAY – JUNE	30 days	9th	3rd
TAMMUZ	JUNE – JULY	29 days	10th	4th
AB	JULY – AUG.	30 days	11th	5th
ELUL	AUG. – SEPT.	29 days	12th	6th

Lesson One

Chapters One and Two
"A Dangerous Trio"

"Pride goes before destruction, a haughty spirit before a fall." Proverbs 16:18

CHAPTER ONE
Read chapter one now . . .

Pride, wine, and wrath, certainly are a dangerous trio; and we will witness their effects on the powerful king and his subjects, who suffer from their affects too. Because this man will not be ruled by God, he will be overruled by God! We can work with God—or we can be *worked* by God.

As we begin reading Esther chapter one, we learn that this is the third year of Ahasuerus' reign. Ahasuerus is a relatively new king and he is preparing himself, and his kingdom for war. His lavish entertainment of princes, nobles, and army officers of Persia and Media is an attempt to garner their support by demonstrating that he can afford the cost of this military action. Greece is his target, according to Greek historian Herodotus, and Greece is a very lofty target!

1. Can you think of other practical reasons that may explain the six months of *lavish display* by Ahasuerus?

2. What personal observations do you make about the king through this lavish display?

3. Preparation is critical for success. Ahasuerus prepares for success with things from this world: money, influence, and power. In contrast, how does the Christian prepare for success?

4. Record the "godly success points" you find next to each of the following verses:

- Proverbs 3:5-6

- Proverbs 16:7

- Philippians 2:5-7

- Mark 9:35

Ahasuerus doesn't just want to succeed; Ahasuerus wants to be *a success!* You may wonder, "What's wrong with success, shouldn't we want to be successful?" There is nothing wrong with wanting to be successful at your endeavors and especially endeavors for the Lord. In fact, we should desire to do/be our *utmost for His Highest.* However, there is a difference between wanting to *succeed* and wanting to be *a success.* This is the distinguishing difference: pride *drives* us—while humility *leads* us!

5. Consider your own desires for success: are you being *driven,* or are you being *led?*

Do you struggle with wanting to be successful? Sometimes, or even often times, we measure success differently than God does. We may pray diligently and follow God wholly on a project, and yet still experience failure. This type of experience can cause us to scratch our heads—but maybe God is doing exactly what He wants to do! God can use this type of experience to develop your gifts, purify your motives, deepen your faith, strengthen your patience; and God can use this type of experience to answer the deepest prayer of your heart! Ultimately, God will always take opportunity to add to your character; leading you to greater humility and dependence on Him. So really, *failure* can be success! It's all about perspective!

6. If you can recall a time when this was your experience, briefly record what you gained:

7. All of us struggle with wanting to be a success in one way or another, and in varying degrees. But for the Christian, this can amount to pride, which is sin. Once we recognize this is a *sin factor*, it actually takes the weight off, because we can confess our sin and leave our "success" in the hands of the Lord! Record your thoughts on this and be as candid as possible. Be prepared to share your thoughts about this during group discussion:

> *"It is more than comforting to realize that it is those who plumbed the depths of failure to whom God invariably gives the call to shepherd others....Without a bitter experience of their own inadequacy and poverty they are quite unfitted to bear the burden of spiritual ministry."*
> J. C. Metcalfe

8. Success within ministry can be very tricky! Sometimes it is a very fine line which separates *successful* ministry and *self-realization!* What did Jesus say about successful ministry in Luke 10:17-20? (Take special note of "who" Jesus saw fall when He was addressing successful ministry!)

Queen Vashti is requested by the drunken king to wear her royal crown and display her beauty before all of the leaders, who presumably are drinking too. She refuses. Who can blame her? *Then the king became very angry and his wrath burned within him.* (Verses 9-12)

It has been said, "When wine goes in—wisdom goes out!" Ahasuerus certainly is a classic example of this statement! When a person drinks alcohol, they are *under the influence* of the alcohol. Their thoughts, decisions, and reactions are under the influential power of alcohol instead of the influential power of the Holy Spirit. Scripture tells us that we should not *get drunk with wine, for that is dissipation, but be filled with the Spirit.* (Ephesians 5:18) "Dissipation" is defined: *to become scattered, disperse, dispel, overindulgence, squandering of resources, wasteful, abating of feeling or emotion.*

Christians need concentrated power—not diluted power! Don't waste or squander your spiritual resources. Christians should never be under the influence of *anything* which can dispel, abate, or dull the voice and the subtle promptings of the Holy Spirit. We need to be sharp and ready for action, especially today! Jesus said, *"But I say to you, I will not drink of this fruit of the vine from now on until that day when I drink it new with you in My Father's kingdom."* (Matthew 26:29) Perhaps this last Word can simplify the matter for you if you struggle with this topic—*"I will not drink . . ."*

9. Avoiding the debate whether Christians have the liberty to drink alcohol, we should simply ask ourselves these questions: "Do I feel more spiritually connected to the Lord; sharp and ready for opportunities to share my faith, ready for spiritual warfare, or ready for any spiritual ministry at all—if I am *under the influence* of any type of intoxicating substance?"

      a. What makes a Christian sharp and ready? (See Matthew 26:41, Acts 1:8, Romans 12:1-2, Galatians 5:16, 2 Timothy 3:14)

      b. Read 1 Corinthians 10:23, and 1 Peter 5:8. How do these verses apply to this topic?

      c. PERSONAL: What is your conclusion?

      For this section of the lesson you'll need to use your spiritual magnifying glass; look for *God Unseen!*

10. Verse 12 gives you a secret view of a man's heart, what do you see? How can the writer of Esther know what is in Ahasuerus' heart? (See Genesis 18:15, Matthew 9:4, 12:25, Luke 9:47)

11. Using a dictionary, note the distinguishing differences between: "anger" and "wrath."

12. What does the king do next, from verse 13?

13. What advice is the king given, and what is the new *law*, from verse 19?

14. What special insight does Proverbs 16:14 give you?

MEMORY VERSE: *"Pride goes before destruction, a haughty spirit before a fall."* Proverbs 16:18

CHAPTER TWO

Read chapter two now . . .

"After these things . . ." Nearly four years pass since Vashti refuses the king's request. During this time the king goes to war attempting to conquer Greece. According to Herodotus, the Persian king loses his military campaign very badly. Retreat is the only military action to the overwhelming advantage of the Greeks. It is a defeated Ahasuerus who returns to the palace. That too, is all part of the providence of God! Ahasuerus will not become the ruling power of the world. In fact, the power shift is now set in motion in favor of the Greeks; and this deep disappointment will help Ahasuerus see that he needs a new queen . . .

The dangerous trios of pride, wine, and wrath have run their course. It is easy to follow the progression: pride leads to an over indulgence of alcohol—the effects of alcohol lead to a lack of self-control, which lead to a foolish request, which lead to uncontrolled anger—wrath!

Anger can result in terrible consequences. Wrath *always* results in terrible consequences! The anger which "burned" within the king's heart in the Hebrew is: *brutish, to kindle, to set on fire.* Even though Scripture tells us that the king's anger has subsided, *he remembers Vashti, and what she has done.* Wrath can subside, as is the case with the king—but it is far from gone. His wrath can be ignited once again in the right circumstances. That's the problem with wrath; it may subside—but at the smallest provocation can erupt into a violent volcano spewing damage everywhere it touches!

1. Read, record, and meditate on what these Scripture verses say about anger:

- Ecclesiastes 7:9

- Matthew 5:21-26

- Ephesians 4:26

- 1 Timothy 2:8

Do you ever have concerns that you may have a problem with anger? If you aren't sure, ask those who live with you! A lot of denial and even shame can be associated with issues of anger, wrath, or rage, especially for the Christian. If you are suffering in this way please seek someone that you respect and who is very mature in the Lord, who will partner in prayer with you, and hold you accountable. Don't ignore this issue! You, and those who love you, don't need to live this way. Get an action plan started. There is hope and healing in the Lord! S E L A H . . .

It's important to know that approximately 50,000 Jews return to Jerusalem, and approximately 1.5 million Jews remain in voluntary exile. Why? Apparently the Jews that remain become very comfortable. They marry, have families, build homes, and even have ways of providing for themselves. This is where we find Mordecai and his cousin, Hadassah, or Esther. Why doesn't Mordecai return to Jerusalem while he can? Perhaps this is another glimpse of *God Unseen?* Is God influencing the thoughts of Mordecai and creating circumstances which cause Mordecai to remain in Susa, *for such a time as time as this?* Whatever the reasons—God is certainly helping Himself to every person and every situation in the book of Esther!

It would be interesting for you to turn to Jeremiah chapter 29 now, and read verses 1–13. God gave instructions about exile living; and He gave His beloved people a very special promise, which has become the anthem for Christians to this very day!

2. From verse 5, we learn that Mordecai is a Benjamite. Do some digging by using the resources you have: a concordance, topical index, or Bible commentary; and record a few notable points that you discover about the tribe of Benjamin:

3. What New Testament writer is also from the tribe of Benjamin? (See Philippians chapter three.)

Esther is chosen as one of the young virgins which will be presented to the king. She finds favor and is transferred to a special location in the harem . . . and so Esther begins the lengthy series of cosmetics and special diet. Remember, Esther is a young woman who is orphaned as a girl; experiencing deep heartache that most can only imagine. No doubt Esther misses the tender love of her mother and father, and now she is to be presented to a man who seems incapable of true love; his heart is full of lust! The word "loved" from verse 17 in the Hebrew is: *to have affection for sexually, or as a friend.*

A year has passed during the preparations, Esther's time has come. She is given instructions by Hegai, and she is also given instructions by Mordecai—she follows instructions by both . . .

4. What instructions does Mordecai give Esther, and why do you think he does so, from verse 10?

5. What notable trait do you see in Esther, from verse 15?

6. Using the Jewish calendar on page 13, what is the corresponding month indicated in verse 16?

7. From verse 17, what is the outcome?

8. From verses 11 and 15, where can Mordecai be found during this time?

9. *". . . Esther did what Mordecai told her as she had done when under his care."* (Verse 20) Esther clearly has developed the habit of obedience. We all have a "go-to" reaction when asked to do something, and so it is our habit: to obey or to disobey. What's your "go-to" reaction—what's your habit, when you are asked to do something by someone in any type of authority?

10. Habits are important! Good habits can make us—and bad habits can break us! This is a good time to consider both. Being very honest with yourself:

    a. Make a short list of your good habits:

    b. Now make a short list of your bad habits:

11. Does the good *outweigh* the bad?

> *The most important habit you can develop is simply to say "Yes, LORD."*
>
> *This simple habit can change your entire life! You can be one "YES" away from a totally different life!*
>
> S e l a h

Turning Point Prayer

"The battle of prayer is against two things in the earthlies: wandering thoughts and lack of intimacy with God's character as revealed in His word. Neither can be cured at once, but they can be cured by discipline."

Oswald Chambers

This can be *your* turning point prayer! Why should you, the people who love you, or the people who work with you, suffer from your bad habits? Why not ask the Lord to help you change your bad habits? You are being challenged to take steps today which can result in change! These may be small, large, or even drastic steps! Maybe you need to simply walk away from the triggers: change your routine, avoid certain places and people. Ask the Lord what you can do to affect real change in your life—He will show you! Only be sincere, and be ready to respond! This really can be *your turning point prayer!* Record what the Lord shows you:

ONE MORE THING . . . read verses 21-23 now.

This can be *your* turning point prayer! Mordecai thwarts an assassination attempt on the king. His name is only recorded; he is not given any special recognition or reward. But God knows! God sees! At the most advantageous moment God will lift the veil on Mordecai's good deed! Have you been overlooked for some good deed? Perhaps it is even something you put a lot of effort into, and someone else got the credit? Is your heart hurt and is your heart in jeopardy of becoming hardened as a result? Record what Galatians 6:9 tells you. Will you record a prayer which expresses your trust in the Lord with this experience?

NOTES

Lesson Two

Chapters Three and Four

"Choices"

". . . Choose for yourselves today whom you will serve . . . as for me and my house, we will serve the Lord." Joshua 24:15

CHAPTER THREE

Read chapter three now . . .

A king chooses a queen—and a queen chooses a destiny . . . and God is in and above it all! In the following study, the providence of God will continue to be made manifest through people unaware. J. Vernon McGee has described the providence of God in this way, *"Providence is the way God leads the man who will not be led."* It is a play on words for sure, but the point is well made! Mordecai and Esther appear to be being led by the providence of God, as there is no mention of their calling on the name of the Lord in Scripture. They may have, but Scripture has omitted it, if it is so. Either way, *God will accomplish all His purposes*, and *no plan of His can be thwarted!*

Chapter three begins with these words, *"After these events . . ."* Another four years pass and suddenly Haman is introduced by the writer. Apparently Haman already is in an important position and presumably highly valued by the king. Haman may even be some type of political advisor. He certainly must be known for his allegiance, support, and like-mindedness to the king to receive this type of promotion. This promotion gives Haman power and authority next to the king, which is a very dangerous combination for this man! The promotion of Haman seems very odd in light of Mordecai's recent valor. It appears Scripture is making a point without making one! God is unseen, but He is working . . .

1. This is our first introduction to Haman—he is an Agagite. He is a descendent of king Agag of the Amalekites; the enemies of the Jews. Describe the power and the authority which is given to Haman, from verses 1-2:

2. Now turn to 1 Samuel 15, and read verses 1-11.

      a. Record the exact command, from verse 3:

      b. Now record what actually happens, from verse 9:

      Partial obedience is disobedience. If Saul obeys fully, there will be no descendants left of Agag, and Haman will not become a clear and present danger to the Jews. Verse 9, alludes that not all are killed, and so there are descendants of Agag. Since Haman exists—we can easily connect the dots that there are survivors. Agag himself is eventually slain by none other than Samuel. The prophet Samuel does the dirty work of the disobedient military leader, King Saul! That's what can happen when we disobey God; often times someone else must deal with our mess, suffer the consequences, and do what we did not do!

> *"Does the LORD delight in burnt offerings and sacrifices as much as in obeying the LORD? To obey is better than sacrifice, and to heed is better than the fat of rams."*
> 1 Samuel 15:22

      Mordecai is a descendant of Saul—Haman is a descendant of Agag. Almost six hundred years later and the descendants of Saul and Agag collide once again . . .

3. It is easy to say that obedience to God is of the utmost importance. But your obedience to God is only as important to you as your reality! Rate your obedience on a scale of 1-10: ten being the most obedient. Circle the number which corresponds to your level of obedience:

     1   2   3   4   5   6   7   8   9   10

      a. Is there room for improvement?

b. Becoming more compliant to God's voice is actually simple! Just do it! Don't complicate obedience with debate. The moment you begin to debate you will side either with the flesh, or worse, with the devil! God is not going to ask you to do something you can't do—it may be something you don't want to do, but it will be within your capabilities. Is He speaking just now? Is there something that God is ministering to you through the course of this study? If so, record briefly what that is, and what action you intend to take:

 One of the saddest commentaries in Scripture is found in 1 Samuel 8:6-9. Read it and weep! The story which we are studying presently may not even exist, if God's people had a different heart then! Consider your story; there is still time for you to make necessary adjustments that He may be highlighting presently! Don't waste your opportunities; guard carefully your heart, and especially appreciate that your Heavenly Father really does know best! S E L A H . . .

Haman was filled with rage, as recorded in verse 5. Who does this remind you of? The king himself promoted Haman—apparently kindred spirits! It has been said, "*You can tell a lot about a man by the company he keeps.*"

4. What does 1 Corinthians 15:33 say about the importance of the company a person chooses to keep?

a. Now consider the company you keep: are they pulling you up, or are they pulling you down?

b. Turning the question around: what type of company are you? Are you pulling people up, or are you pulling them down?

Haman decides that not only Mordecai needs to die for his "crime," but the entire Jewish population! That certainly is an overreaction and is majorly disproportionate to the *crime*. Just like Ahasuerus, he is an unreasonable man who overreacts to circumstances at hand. However, this is an opportunity for Haman to not only vent, but to exercise his anti-Semitism; to be rid of an entire race of people which he hates!

5. Who do you think is really influencing and driving Haman's rage? Why?

a. Do you think it possible that Haman doesn't even realize why he hates the Jews? What are your thoughts?

b. Record other attempts from Scripture, or other historical resources, to annihilate the Jewish Nation and her people:

6. Using the Jewish calendar on page 13, what is the corresponding month indicated in verse 7?

7. What does Haman promise the king if this is done, from verse 9?

8. The indifferent Ahasuerus tells Haman to do *as he likes* with the silver and the Jews! Later on, you will learn Haman's intentions are to benefit from the plunder of the Jews. Note: by plundering the Jews, the Jews will be financing their own decimation! Answer the following questions, from verses 12-15:

a. On which day is this to happen?

b. What are they to do with the Jews possessions?

c. What are Haman and Ahasuerus doing during this time?

d. What is the reaction in the capital city, Susa?

It is easy to see why the city is in total confusion. "Why kill all the Jews—what have they done? What has changed? Why? The Jews have become our neighbors, friends, work associates—why is there a decree to kill them?" Or, "They've always been an odd people, I don't trust them, I don't like them—I hate them!" Just as it is to this day, there are those who love the Jews, and there are those who hate the Jews. While others want to see them wiped off the face of the earth! All simply because they are Jews!

MEMORY VERSE: *". . . Choose for yourselves today whom you will serve . . . as for me and my house, we will serve the Lord."* Joshua 24:15

CHAPTER FOUR
Read chapter four now . . .

A time for tearing clothes, and a time for wearing sackcloth and ash. A time for weeping, and a time for mourning and fasting. But there is no mention of prayer! Did Mordecai pray? Did the Jews pray? We would assume so, but we simply do not know . . .

1. There is no mention of praying while fasting in Scripture during this time; however, prayer is typically associated with fasting. Many people fast for many reasons—even for "spiritual" reasons, but they are not necessarily praying. If the Jews are praying, the Holy Spirit chose not to record it. What are your thoughts about this?

2. What do the following verses say about God's response to those who call upon His Name?

- Psalm 20:6

- Isaiah 65:24

- Jeremiah 33:3

- Romans 10:13

This is a time in Jewish history when the vast majority of God's own people are not directly seeking His perfect will; they are being *led by God's providence.* Could this resolve the answer why His Name is not mentioned in Esther? Nevertheless, conflict and crisis are often the "goads" which God uses to draw us close to Him and to ignite our spiritual passions! Our loving Heavenly Father provides and He protects, often in spite of us; and He will do whatever is necessary to *get us home safely!* God may be unseen, but He is never absent!

3. There is a difference between God's *perfect will* and His *permissive will.* Are you seeking God's perfect will—or are you drifting through your existence in His permissive will, hoping it all turns out well? What choices are you presently making: *perfect will* or *permissive will?* Explain your conclusions:

4. Are you experiencing *conflict and crisis* in your life right now? Could God be calling you to *ash and sackcloth*—or perhaps the word is *spiritual renewal?* If so, pray for the Holy Spirit to come upon you and to fill you anew! *Return to your first love . . .* (Revelation 2:5). Record your thoughts:

For this section of the lesson you'll need to use your spiritual magnifying glass; look for *God Unseen!*

This is when things really get going in the story of Esther! The providence of God is manifested through the palace maidens and eunuchs. They inform Esther about her cousin Mordecai, as apparently she is unaware of his condition brought on by the deadly decree. As a queen, Esther is isolated from city news while in the palace—so she is perplexed and in anguish to learn about Mordecai's condition, "Why would he be in such a state?" It also appears the maidens and the eunuchs are unaware of the decree, even though they have observed Mordecai's behavior. But this is the point: they *do* notice Mordecai's behavior and appearance, and they *do* something about it! Whatever their motives are, their actions make all the difference! Perhaps more evidence of *God Unseen?*

5. Where is Mordecai located during this time, from verse 2?

6. Recall and record when Mordecai is previously seen at this location:

7. What is the reason Mordecai can go no further?

Mordecai can only go as far as the gate; he cannot *enter* the king's gate. Previously, Mordecai is seen *sitting at the king's gate.* This denotes his position as either a political figure or some time type of judge—it most definitely is a position of some importance.

8. In detail, describe everything that Mordecai says and gives to Hathach, from verses 7 and 8:

9. What is Esther's reply, from verse 11?

10. Without consideration of the end of this story, what is your impression of Esther at this point?

11. How long has it been since Esther has seen the king?

12. Do you think Esther comprehends the magnitude of the situation? Record your thoughts and be prepared to share them in group discussion:

"And they related Esther's words to Mordecai." Mordecai's response records some of the most beloved words in all of Scripture—we love to read and quote his words. But these are really hard words, powerful words, choice words; words which are carefully prepared in Mordecai's mind. Ultimately, these are Divine words, prepared by *God Unseen!* Each and every word counts! The stakes are high, every word must hit their target—Esther's heart!

13. Record e v e r y word Mordecai tells Hathach to say to Esther, from verse 13:

14. Record e v e r y word Mordecai tells Hathach to tell Esther, from verse 14:

As noted previously, these are very hard and powerful words. Just imagine if you can, being in Esther's position as she hears these words for the very first time . . . Not only can one hear a pin drop in the room, one can hear her heartbeat as well! The gravity of the situation is finally taking hold, and Esther is beginning to realize that she is the one. She is the only one, who can choose to stand between life or death, *for her father's house, and for herself!*

15. What did Mordecai say will happen for the Jews if Esther chooses not to act, from verse 14?

16. Did you notice that deliverance will come for the Jews, but not necessarily for Esther? Record your thoughts about this?

17. *"And who knows whether you have not attained royalty for such a time as this?"* What is your position? Are you married? Are you a parent? Are you an employer, or are you employed? Are you in ministry? Think about those who depend upon you—what is your responsibility towards them because of your position/s? Record your position/s, and any thoughts the Lord may be stirring in your heart about your responsibilities, and your recent choices:

No other person can do what God is calling <u>you</u> to do with your life. No one can love, care for, and give, to your family in the way that you can. No one can do what you can do within the circle that God has strategically placed you in, wherever that is. No one! Some needs may be met by others—but it will not be the same as when you *fulfill your purpose.* You have a unique call on your life, and only you can fulfill it!

18. Think about opportunities that God has recently presented to you: are you hesitant based upon your perceived inadequacies, fears, or inconveniences? Or, is your response, "No matter what, I will follow Thee, I will act?" Record any new perspectives or thoughts you may have now:

THE GREATEST CHOICE OF ALL . . .

The Christian story is born out of the Jews story. Many attempts by Satan were made to prevent Jesus' advent. But Jesus Christ has come! He has come to the world to save that which is lost. Jesus Christ came, suffered, died, and rose again, so that we could be with Him forever!

If you don't know this Jesus, now is a great time to get to know Him! He already knows you. In fact, He knows all about you, and He loves you anyway! Are you willing to choose Him, just as He chose you? Are you willing to call upon His Name? If so, confess to Him that you know you are a sinner in need of a Savior, and that you believe He is that Savior! If you prayed this way, please share this *good news* with your group, or with some other Christian!

Welcome to the family of God! Heaven is rejoicing in your choice!

Turning Point Prayer

"Around us is a world lost in sin, above us is a God willing and able to save; it is ours to build
the bridge that links heaven and earth, and prayer is the mighty instrument that does the work.
If we do our part, God will do His."

E. M. Bounds

This can be *your* turning point prayer! Obedience can be the one thing that makes all the
difference! Today is the day to turn from what is, and to live the life that God has perfectly planned for
you. For some, it may be some small matter of obedience. For others, it may be one big glaring matter of
obedience—and if you choose to obey you can find yourself on a completely different course; from
God's permissive will to His perfect will! Perhaps even from destruction to restoration!

Maybe you don't want anything to change—and perhaps that is what keeps you from obeying
the voice of the Lord. The choice will always be yours to make, and yours to live with! Record your
thoughts and any transactions made with the Lord:

ONE MORE THING . . . read verses 15-17 now.

This can be *your* turning point prayer! Esther declares a fast for three days and nights. She
makes the ultimate choice; she is willing to die for the cause. Missionary Jim Elliott wrote these words in
his journal, *"He is no fool who gives what he cannot keep to gain what he cannot lose."* Elliott gives
excellent perspective! You may appreciate that Esther really doesn't have a choice, when her
circumstances are stripped down. But God allows her this one glorious opportunity in history, to be *His
shining star!* Are you facing a decision too, that there really is only one choice? This can be your
opportunity to shine too! What do you really have to lose? Pray on this matter, and be willing to be *the
bridge which links heaven and earth.* Record your thoughts/prayers about these verses, Esther's
shinning opportunity, and yours!

Notes

Lesson Three

Chapters Five and Six

"The Third Day"

"Whoever exalts himself shall be humbled; and whoever humbles himself shall be exalted."
Matthew 23:12

CHAPTER FIVE

Read chapter five now . . .

Through elaborate banquets and a desperate and humble heart, Esther sets the stage for her shining opportunity. Meanwhile, Haman sets his own stage through a confident and prideful heart—which will drive him to his own demise! The reader once again gains insight into the private heart of a man; more evidence of *God Unseen* in the book of Esther! As Haman propels himself further down the road of destruction—we realize this man wants more than homage and more than revenge; this man wants blood!

Esther steps forward. It is her appointed day! However, she is not hasty with her request. Esther's request will come when she is absolutely certain that her *time* is come. God is unseen, but very much leading, very much present—God is there!

1. Which day does Esther present herself, from verse 1?

2. What other notable historical event happened on *"the third day?"*

 Esther is a type of Christ: she is willing to sacrifice herself; she is also an advocate for her people as she intercedes on their behalf. That *third day* changed the course set for the Jews! Jesus Christ is our Sacrifice. He is also our Advocate and our Intercessor, (1 Corinthians 5:7, 1 John 2:1, Hebrews 7:25). Jesus died a real death and rose from the dead on the *third day.* Because of that *third day* event, we have a Living Savior who is an Advocate making intercession on our behalf at this very moment! Because of that *third day,* our course is changed forever too!

Make the connection . . . Esther chapter five is rich with symbolism! The following questions only begin the "symbolism" study. If you have time and are so inspired, please continue with your own study using these questions as a guide.

3. Answer the following questions:

    a. What is Esther wearing?

    b. Where is the king seated?

    c. When the king sees Esther, what is his reaction?

4. *Make the connection . . .* record what you discover:

    a. What are you clothed with? See Isaiah 61:10.

    b. Where is Jesus seated? Colossians 3:1.

> *"If Jesus rose from the dead, then you have to accept all that He said; if He didn't rise from the dead, then why worry about any of what He said? The issue on which everything hangs is not whether or not you like His teaching but whether or not He rose from the dead."*
> Timothy Keller

    c. How do you approach Jesus, and how are you received? See Hebrews 4:16, and Ephesians 1:6 (KJV is best for this verse!).

5. THE THIRD DAY: Using a Bible concordance, look up the word "third," and take note of "third day" happenings. For those who have time, this is a very rich study and will most certainly bless! Record a few notable events:

Haman goes out from the presence of the king and queen very pleased with himself. Of all people, the queen invited Haman to attend a private party! Haman is *glad and pleased, in his heart.* The word for "heart" from verse 9, in the Hebrew, refers to: *feelings, the will, even intellect.* Haman is simply in a good mood—but that is about to change! Moods, feelings, and even our intellect, are all subject to change based upon circumstances. However, joy from the Lord is something which remains, even if we're in a bad-sad mood, because His joy is <u>not</u> something which is generated by circumstances—it is given, and given by the Divine. You may not *feel* joyful, but His joy is in you!

6. Record what you learn about godly joy from these verses:

- Nehemiah 8:10

- Psalm 16:11

- John 15:11

- Romans 14:17

- Galatians 5:22

If you're experiencing a time of being low of heart just now, and although He already knows, tell Him how you're feeling anyway. Speak out your heart to Him, and then wait in silence. Give Him time to minister. It is in His presence where you will get back in touch with His joy. Your *feelings* may deceive you, so let Him remind you: His joy is real—and He is with you, you are not alone!

> *"Trust God's Word and His power more than you trust your own feelings and experiences."*
> Samuel Rutherford

7. Haman summons support from his wife and friends—*"misery loves company,"* apparently! As he recounts his wealth, sons, and position, he confesses that they do not satisfy. If only Haman had counted his *blessings* instead of his *possessions* that day! S E L A H . . .

a. What exactly does Haman say about Mordecai, from verse 13?

b. What advice is given to Haman by his wife and friends, and what is Haman's reaction?

MEMORY VERSE: *"Whoever exalts himself shall be humbled; and whoever humbles himself shall be exalted."* Matthew 23:12

CHAPTER SIX

Read chapter six now . . .

A sleepless night, some boring records, and *God Unseen!* Everyone experiences a sleepless night now and again; too much rich food, caffeine and concerns, are all ingredients for a sleepless night for sure—but there appears to be something much more to this sleepless night which the king experiences, for *the king could not sleep.*

1. What is discovered in the chronicles which are read to the king, from verse 2?

      a. What does the king ask the servants?

      b. What is the reply by the servants?

      It has been five years since Mordecai intervened in the assassination plot against the king—and now his day has come! Likewise, the Lord knows about your good deeds too. It's normal to want your good deeds remembered and rewarded. If it is in your best interest, your day will come too—just be patient. When you need it—God will give it.

2. The king just happens to hear someone in the outer court, who is it and what is on his mind?

3. Briefly summarize verses 5-9:

4. From verse 10, how does the king *classify* Mordecai?

      It hardly seems plausible that the king knows Mordecai is a Jew, and yet at the same time has an active decree calling for the annihilation of all the Jews! Ahasuerus is a careless man and a careless leader. When a person is careless they will often suffer the consequences of their carelessness. When a person is careless and in any type of leadership; including in the home, others will suffer from their carless ways. It is important to note that absentmindedness is not necessarily carelessness, or sinfulness. But one should distinguish which is their problem and take steps to remedy it.

5. The king wants to honor the Jew—the evil servant wants to murder the Jew! Two rival powers: God versus Satan! How are Satan and God contrasted in John 10:10?

> "'No weapon that is formed against you will prosper; and every tongue that accuses you in judgment you will condemn. This is the heritage of the servants of the Lord, and their vindication is from Me,' declares the Lord." (Isaiah 54:17)

6. Record the words which Haman is forced to proclaim as he parades Mordecai on horseback through the city square:

7. Some would call this "poetic justice," what does the Bible say is really happening? See Galatians 6:7:

It is easy to become distraught when wronged—but God knows, and God sees, and if He wants to make it right, He can do so in an instant. If this is your present experience, remember what your heritage is, and give God time. If you're alive to be reading this lesson—that means it's not over. You haven't lived the last paragraph of the last chapter of your story yet. If God still has time—so do you!

8. In what condition is Haman when he returns home?

a. For contrast, where does Mordecai go immediately after being honored?

Mordecai goes right back to his position—in other words, he goes back to work. It can actually be a precarious time immediately following the experience of commendation. The temptation might be to go home and celebrate; gloat and get puffed up. But that's not what Mordecai does. No, he goes right back to work! S E L A H . . .

9. Record, and be ready to share, any personal experiences which you may have had that align with this topic. Did you resist celebrating, or did you bask in your moment of favor?

For this section of the lesson you'll need to use your spiritual magnifying glass; look for *God Unseen!*

10. Chapter six of Esther records several events which reveal *God Unseen.* List them as you <u>see</u> them. (Hint: Verse 6 is not previously addressed in this lesson. However, it contains one of the most obvious evidence's of *God Unseen!*)

"During the night the king could not sleep . . ." Ahasuerus certainly does not present as a believer in the God of Abraham, Isaac, and Jacob. But God is beginning to work through his life, even though he is not a seemingly willing participant. God will protect and spare His people—but God is also protecting and sparing Ahasuerus from committing a horrific crime by being responsible for murdering the Jews, and from sinning against Him in this way! For another beautiful account of a man God spared from shedding blood, read 1 Samuel 25:2-39.

God is sparing us more than we know, and it won't be until that day when we are *face to face,* that we'll know just exactly how many times! It is His nature to spare all of His children from committing foolish and costly mistakes, if only we will listen. God has spared—because God loves! In fact, His love is so great that He did <u>not</u> spare His own Son, just so He <u>could</u> spare YOU!

11. If you can recall a time when you knew without a doubt that God intervened, and caused you to change course, sparing you from doing something you would have seriously regretted, record what you gained in spiritual understanding:

God is working in the heart of the king; *He turns it wherever He wishes,* and so we are gaining hope that things are about to change drastically in our story . . .

12. What prophetic words does Zeresh say to Haman, from verse 13?

Turning Point Prayer

"If our hopes are being disappointed just now, it means that they are being purified . . . One of the greatest strains in life is the strain of waiting for God, 'Because thou hast kept the word of My patience.' Remain spiritually tenacious."
Oswald Chambers

This can be *your* turning point prayer! Are you experiencing a time of disappointment just now? Are you praying and believing that God is leading you towards a certain opportunity, only now it is falling away? Resist the temptation to sulk, or *cover your head,* as Haman did. Dear blessed one of the Lord, you must trust that He knows what is best. The opportunity may still remain, and is simply being kept safe in your future! Will you be faithful to remain spiritually tenacious? This is not the time to turn down the flame on your prayers. No, keep them hot! Keep your prayers boiling hot! If the Lord continues to say, "No," then that's exactly what you want, too. You don't want anything that He doesn't want for you. As you turn this way in prayer, record any new thoughts you may have—even those which may seem small and of little significance:

ONE MORE THING . . . read James 3:13-18.

This can be *your* turning point prayer! Jealousy can be a hard thing to pin down—it is the sensitive soul who hears the voice of the Lord saying, "That is just simple jealousy. Confess it. Let it go. It will only hurt you." Haman had many issues, one of which was jealousy, and any Bible study student can easily diagnose this. However, it is much more difficult to self-diagnose. Are you willing to ask the Lord if there be any tones of jealousy within you? Don't ignore it, and don't be embarrassed by it. Just deal with it. This is an excellent time for you to prayerfully take care of this matter!

Notes

Lesson Four

Chapters Seven and Eight

"Exposed"

"But there is nothing covered up that will not be revealed, and hidden that will not be known."
Luke 12:2

CHAPTER SEVEN

Read chapter seven now . . .

It is very difficult to be aware of an evil deed while waiting and hoping for justice. But God knows. God sees. God is on the Throne—and God is just! At just the right time, what is hidden will be uncovered; Esther will expose the evil plot of Haman. The irony of events is unmistakable—beginning with Haman's false sense of security because of his position under the king! The irony being that Mordecai warns Esther that she should not presume herself safe just because she is in the king's palace, and so she does not. But it appears Haman never considers the possibility that he himself can be in danger . . .

Haman feels safe, secure, and powerful. Haman presumes the power and authority which are granted to him are "rights" instead of "responsibilities." Haman also doesn't feel a sense of responsibility to accurately represent facts to the king (Esther 3:8). The king relies and depends on Haman to be accurate when he reports to him about kingdom business. But God knows who He is working with—a foolish king, and an evil conniving liar with high ambition!

1. What do you suppose may be Haman's high ambition? Reference, Esther 6:6-9.

The fantasy plays out perfectly in Haman's own mind—but, *"Pride goes before destruction, a haughty spirit before a fall."* In one day, the fantasy of exaltation will turn into calamity! *". . . the king's eunuchs arrived and hastily brought Haman to the banquet."*

2. At the banquet of wine, the king revisits his earlier question to the queen; his intrigue is peaked and Esther senses this is her appointed opportunity! What does the king conclude his question with, from verse 2?

Note: The statement made by the king, *"even to half of the kingdom,"* is a royal promise that is not meant to be taken literally, (i.e. Daniel 5:16, Mark 6:23). This statement only means that the king will be very generous. The king knows the matter on his queen's heart is extremely important to her, for all of her elaborate preparations. Now the king's curiosity will be satisfied—the queen gives him her requests . . .

3. Esther prefaces her request with an attitude of respect. It is always wise to demonstrate respect to those who are in authority. What two key phrases does Esther use to demonstrate her respect to the king?

4. If the Lord has placed authority over you that is lacking in character and wisdom, your struggle is real. But again, God knows who He is working with—and you don't know whether or not you have been placed in your situation, *for such a time as this.* What do these verses say about respect and authority?

- Exodus 20:12

- Psalm 75:7

- 1 Peter 2:13-15

- 1 Peter 3: 1-3

5. Can you recall a time when you knew that you were given favor because of your respectful behavior? Record a few words; including a Scripture verse if you had one, and be prepared to share your experience with your group. This can be a time of great encouragement!

6. Unlike Haman, Esther is very accurate when relaying information to the king. Record the details she gives the king about this threat, from verse 4:

7. Esther makes a distinction between her desperate request and what the king may consider an "annoyance." Being sold into slavery hardly seems an "annoyance," but Esther has *bigger fish to fry!* Can Esther be highlighting the magnitude of this situation by making this comparison? What are your thoughts?

> *". . . How idiotic I have been! I was forgetting about our gracious God,*
> *Who said, 'you believe you are about to be abandoned? Don't be silly!*
> *No, things will not go as you think.'"*
> Victor Hugo
> Les Miserables

The king probably assumes the queen is Persian, but now he finds out differently. The light is beginning to dawn . . . the king is in bit of an embarrassing situation, "who are your people, Esther?"—begs the question! But it is a question not asked. Instead, Ahasuerus wants to know where the threat is originating from, *"who is he, and where is he, who would presume to do this?"*

8. Can you imagine the fear which is gripping Haman as he is listening to this dialogue between the king and the queen? Based on what you know already about Haman, what thoughts do you think are going through his mind?

9. The Lord is gracious and slow to anger. He is also patient, and desires that all would come to repentance (Psalm 103:8, 2 Peter 3:9). God gives Haman time—more than enough time; to repent and to right his wrongs. But Haman will not! What does Numbers 32:23 say?

 Is the Holy Spirit bringing a sin to mind? Do you think it's time to take care of it? Don't waste this opportunity. Don't harden your heart! By heeding the prompting of the Holy Spirit at this very moment, you can allow God to spare you from something terrible, even from something devastating!

We can only imagine the kings' shock once he connects the dots: his queen is a Jew and her life is in danger—and he signed her death warrant! While the king is incensed that someone presumes to threaten the queen's life, it also seems the king is indifferent to the Jews in general. He appears unaffected by the anti-Semitic atmosphere in Persia. He neither loves the Jews nor hates the Jews; but now he is forced to act—because now it's personal! God made it personal! God is unseen, but God is pinning the king down. The king must act on His Sovereign behalf to not only save the queen, but to save His people!

10. What does Matthew 12:30 say?

 11. It is very important for Christians to appreciate the special place the Jews hold in the heart of God. Be reminded of God's promise to His chosen people now. Please read and record Genesis 12:3:

The king is enraged that someone would presume to kill his queen, especially to find out that it is his right-hand man, Haman! In the king's mind—he has been betrayed; betrayed by a man he trusted! A man placed within his own privacy; given privilege, prestige, and power! So the king stomps out and into the palace garden, probably to get some fresh air to help him sober up. The king needs to think; he needs all of his wits about him. To add insult to injury, the person who normally would advise him during such a crisis, is the would-be assassin!

11. Haman is terrified; he knows what is about to happen to him! Where is he found when the king returns?

Apparently Haman doesn't know Mordecai is a relative of the queen. Before ordering an execution of such magnitude it would seem reasonable to order equivalent investigations. Perhaps even a simple investigation would have revealed the relational facts. Either way, his plot is not well thought out. Hatred and revenge have a way of taking reasonable thinking and logic out of the equation!

12. Haman's pleas for intervention by the queen are *misunderstood* by the king. Knowing the queen has already implicated Haman as an assassin; do you believe the king really thinks Haman is trying to assault the queen with the eunuchs present? Or, do you think the king uses this immediate scenario as a *scapegoat?*

13. The eunuchs hear it all, so they cover the face of Haman—he has dishonored the king and queen, judgment is inescapable . . .

    a. What *special character trait* is noted by Harbonah about Mordecai, which he relates to the king at this time, from verse 9?

    b. What order does Ahasuerus give, and how does he feel afterward, from verse 10?

MEMORY VERSE: *"But there is nothing covered up that will not be revealed, and hidden that will not be known."* Luke 12:2

CHAPTER EIGHT

Read chapter eight now . . .

Haman is no longer personally a threat, he is dead—but his threats still remain very much alive: *to destroy, to kill, to annihilate all the Jews, and plunder their possessions.* There remains one more request by the queen . . .

1. On which day does the king give Haman's house to the Queen, from verse 1?

      a. How is Haman described?

      b. What does the queen disclose to the king about Mordecai?

2. Who is in possession of the king's signet ring now, from verse 2?

      a. Who does Esther set over her new house, from verse 2?

3. Esther once again speaks to the king; she mentions nothing of herself, it's all about her people, the Jews. What a transformation! When Mordecai first brought this crisis to Esther's attention, what was her primary concern? (See Esther 4:11)

4. Describe Esther's posture: her emotions, and what she does before the king, from verse 3?

      God has done something very special for Esther; she remembers who she is! She now completely identifies as a Jew. She has grown in her understanding, and she has matured spiritually. She so identifies with her people and purpose that her personal safety doesn't mean what it once did. Esther has new vision! Esther recognizes her special and unique position. She is not just a beauty queen; she is valued and valuable—she is the chief intercessor for her people, *for such a time as this!*

5. The king extends the golden scepter . . . now Esther will be very specific in her request. What does Esther ask the king to do about the decree, from verse 5?

6. From verse 6, what can Esther not endure? What can you infer about Esther's own situation, from this statement?

Esther now stands before the king and lays out the details, once again. Though Esther is filled with emotion, she composes herself and returns to her former respectful and formal behavior as she appeals to the king on behalf of her people . . .

7. From verse 7, we're given insight about the king's decision to hang Haman. What reason does the king give for hanging Haman? (Do you remember the king's accusation in Esther 7:8?)

It is amazing that it has only been two months since the original decree was signed! Mordecai will be responsible for overseeing the new decree. The decree is to be translated in every language for each of the provinces, and to all the Jews in their own language . . .

Use the Jewish calendar on page 13 to answer the following questions:

8. What is the corresponding month indicated in verse 9?

9. What does the king grant to the Jews, from verse 11, and what are the Jews told they can do, from verse 13?

10. What is the corresponding month indicated in verse 12?

11. How much time the do the Jews have to prepare for the attack? (See verses 9 and 12)

For this section of the lesson you'll need to use your spiritual magnifying glass; look for *God Unseen!*

12. Verses 15-17 describe the new *heart* condition of the Jews and the celebrations. Then something truly amazing happens! *"Many among the peoples of the land became Jews, for the dread of the Jews had fallen on them."* Describe what you think is occurring, and record any thoughts you have about what God is accomplishing through this horrific threat on His people. (You may also want to read Isaiah 56:6-8 to gain an appreciation for the heart of God towards the foreigner!)

Turning Point Prayer

"…I saw underneath the altar the souls of those who had been slain because of the word of God, and because of the testimony which they had maintained; and they cried out with a loud voice, saying, 'How long, O Lord, holy and true, will You refrain from judging and avenging our blood on those who dwell on the earth?'"

Revelation 6:9-10

Persecution today against the Church is at an all-time high—it is a crisis! But is the Church wearing *sackcloth and ash?* Is there a *loud outcry* by the Church in public and in public forums equivalent to the crisis? Is the Church *pleading* before civic servants in high places? Is the Church *pleading* before her King? Is the Church reacting to the crisis as the Jews did in the book of Esther? This is a message to the Church: *"Do not imagine that you in the king's palace can escape any more than all the Jews."* Esther 4:13 S E L A H …

This can be *your* turning point prayer! Below is a list of the top 10 countries that persecute Christians, according to World Watch List© 2015. The persecutions range from not being able to own Bibles, publicly share their faith and proselytize, to: imprisonment, beatings, stoning's, torture, rape, and murder. What might God do, if His people made this matter the highest priority? What might God do, if His Church got bold and flexed her privilege and power? What might God do, if His Church prayed with fasting for the persecuted Church?

This is personal: Can you pray with fasting one day this week for your brothers and sisters in Christ who are suffering and dying? This can be *their* turning point prayer!

"Pray for us." 1 Thessalonians 5:25

1. North Korea	6. Sudan
2. Somalia	7. Iran
3. Iraq	8. Pakistan
4. Syria	9. Eritrea
5. Afghanistan	10. Nigeria

Notes

Lesson Five

Chapters Nine and Ten

"Things Hoped For"

"Now faith is the substance of things hoped for, the evidence of things not seen."
Hebrews 11:1

CHAPTER NINE

Read chapter nine, verses 1-11 now . . .

The book of Esther is truly an amazing story of divine deliverance through divine actions of an unseen God! While *we* see Him clearly through this miraculous story—He remains "unseen" in the record of Scripture.

It also is a story about a people who grow in their faith through *things hoped for!* The Persians have the overwhelming advantage: power, political leverage, resources—and they have the numbers. But the Jews have an unseen God willing and ready to act! The Jews have only one hope really—and that is, that God will intervene and save them! For what can the Jews do to defend themselves against such an overwhelming enemy?

Even though Haman is dead, the threat remains, because there are other "Haman's" alive and full of his type of hatred for the Jews! We can only imagine what the months are like for the Jews living in Susa and the provinces of Persia . . . possibly jibes and verbal threats, even advantages taken and generalized abuses are suffered by the Jews from their enemies. But *God Unseen* is on the scene! Things are about to change for the Jews in a very dramatic way! Who can predict what is about to happen? The power shift is already taking place . . . *things hoped for* are about to happen!

The new decree is critical and does more than allow the Jews to defend themselves, in whatever manner they need. It also communicates a powerful message to all of Persia that the king does not approve of the annihilation of the Jews. The new decree will be the vehicle which God will use to protect and preserve His beloved people!

1. Verse 1, tells us the new decree is to be executed in the twelfth month, which is Adar, on the thirteenth day. Using the Jewish calendar on page 13, what is the corresponding month?

2. From verse 1, who *hoped to gain mastery over the Jews?*

      a. What actually happens?

 God has a way of turning laws, plans, threats, events, and even hearts, towards His advantage! God can change any situation in an instant! It was Joseph, who said, *". . . you meant evil against me, but God meant it for good in order to bring about this present result, to preserve many people alive."* (Genesis 50:20) This is the history of the Jews! Constant threat of annihilation—and constant deliverances by God! God turns the disadvantage to the advantage!

Note: While reading Scripture it is important to pause periodically, to *Selah*, and think about what you are reading. Remember, the book of Esther records events which take place over the course of ten years, even though it reads as if the events take place over one week or two.

      For this section of the lesson you'll need to use your spiritual magnifying glass; look for *God Unseen!*

3. The Jews are prepared; they are ready for the day! *"No one could stand before them, for the dread of them had fallen on all the peoples."* (Esther 9:2) This is very dramatic! Take some time and ponder what this means. Imagine what this must look like in real-time!

a. How do you imagine the Jews intimidate their attackers?

b. Do you imagine that *God Unseen* is simply prevailing upon the enemies of the Jews by shattering their confidence, fumbling their combat skills, and foiling their battle plans? Or, can it simply be that God is putting a *fear* of the Jews in the hearts of their enemies?

Note: Bible commentators do not agree on what is actually taking place in regards to the *"dread which had fallen upon the people."* But this is what we do know: something supernatural occurs which can only be attributed to God!

4. Who is assisting the Jews, from verses 3-4?

a. Why are they assisting the Jews?

b. God does something truly amazing for all of the Jews, but Mordecai seems to receive a *double portion!* What does verse 4 say about Mordecai?

5. To enhance your understanding about how God feels about His "underdogs," read 1 Corinthians 1:26-29.

a. What type of people does God typically choose?

b. Why does God choose people like this?

c. Do these Scripture verses minister to you today? Record a few words which describe your thoughts about what you have just read:

"Mordecai was great in the king's house, and his fame spread throughout all the provinces, for the man Mordecai became greater and greater." (Esther 9:4) Everyone experiences some type of transformation in this story, including the people who become Jews! Mordecai is easy to admire—but he also undergoes transformation. The reader's observation about his transformation is primarily through his promotions by the king. But those promotions come about only because Mordecai has extraordinary convictions, which are only fortified over time. He is the only man who does not bow or pay homage to Haman!

> *"The greatest challenge in receiving great things from God is holding on for the last half hour."*
> Streams In The Desert

The story might end right here, if only Mordecai will loosen his grip on his convictions! It would be so much easier if he does, right? But God being unseen, is very much present in the details of Mordecai's convictions; in his thoughts, and in his heart. God has much bigger plans for Mordecai as he goes from being the number one man on a hit list—to the second most powerful man in Persia . . .

Transformation: Things Hoped For!

6. If you are presently being pressed towards compromising your godly convictions, how can Mordecai's uncompromising convictions encourage you? Record your thoughts and date this. You may look back at this date someday and be reminded of your faithfulness—and God's faithfulness; to honor your uncompromising convictions!

    a. How does Hebrews 10:35-36, minister to you on this topic?

7. What is revealed about the hearts' of the enemies of the Jews, from verse 5?

    a. How many do the Jews kill in the capital city of Susa? See verses 6 and 15, for the sum number killed.

8. Who else do they kill, from verse 10?

9. What do the Jews not do, from verse 10?

10. Who receives the report on this event, from verse 11?

MEMORY VERSE: *"Now faith is the substance of things hoped for, the evidence of things not seen."* Hebrews 11:1

Read chapter nine, verses 12-16 now . . .

Even Ahasuerus experiences a type of transformation! When first reading about Ahasuerus, he is a drunk given over to making foolish and dangerous decisions; signing decrees without any real understanding or consideration for their consequences! After reading chapter nine, verses 12 – 16, there is a sense that this man experiences some type of transformation. He seems more engaged with the affairs of his kingdom, and his wife. He appears more mature in his appreciation of his unique position as king of Persia—and the role of his queen, and her cousin. He also takes notice that the Jews are special, *"What then have they done in the rest of the king's provinces!"* (Esther 9:12) This is not a question—this is a statement made by a man who is completely and thoroughly impressed by the Jews!

We all have difficult people in our lives, even difficult people which are in positions of authority. What we need to remember is this: all of us are on this side of eternity! It may be a long and difficult course to continually interact or live with such a person/s. But we don't know when it can be *the last half hour!* Perhaps divine deliverance, or divine transformation, is on the way right now!

Transformation: Things Hoped For!

11. If you have such a person, or even persons, in your life, be encouraged and take time now to pray for them. Perhaps more importantly, pray for yourself. Be willing to ask the Lord, "Who is the one who really needs the deliverance or the transformation?" It could just be that both parties are in need!

a. What does Romans 12:17-21 say about difficult relationships?

12. Because the king is seeing something even he cannot explain, what does he do next, from verse 12?

13. Briefly describe Esther's request, and why you think she may have made this particular type of request, from verses 13-15?

We may have thought all of Esther's requests are granted. But the king is intrigued by this entire affair and senses there may be something more. We may need to read between the lines a bit now, perhaps there is a report delivered to Esther that there are more enemies which still remain in Susa, verse 22 seems to suggest this may be the case. There certainly is the matter of Haman's sons to settle.

Note: Verse 13 describes Esther's request that the ten sons of Haman are to be hung on the gallows, while verse 10 tells us they are dead. Verse 10 is the record of the killing of Haman's sons, while verse 13 is the directive by Esther as to what should be done with their bodies. Their bodies hanging on the gallows will certainly serve as a strong deterrent to any who will seek to bring harm to the Jews!

14. What do the Jews not do?

15. How many enemies do the Jews have in the provinces of Persia, from verse 16?

a. What do the Jews not do?

b. How many times does Scripture record that the Jews don't take the plunder?

Read chapter nine, verses 17-32 now . . .

Esther's transformation is the most dramatic for sure! When we read the story of how Esther is brought into the palace, we read it with disdain. We are repulsed by the entire tawdry affair. But we don't read that Esther is! She may be, we simply don't know. It is entirely possible that Esther is infatuated with the king, and the palace lifestyle. After all, she goes from having an ordinary life to living in the palace with all of its glitz and glamor; privilege and power! Can this help to explain the strong coaxing by her cousin, Mordecai, to help her appreciate the gravity of the situation, and her unique opportunity, from chapter four? Remember, Esther is brought into the palace and into her position as queen simply because she is beautiful, and Esther knows this. Above it all, God made Esther beautiful—and God made Ahasuerus appreciate her beauty. More evidence of *God Unseen!*

When Esther is initially informed about her opportunity, her reaction and response is self-motivated; it is all about self-preservation. Who can blame her? The average person is a self-preservationist too! But Esther gets her eyes off of herself and onto her people. When Esther turns her attention to the task at hand, she becomes very sure of herself within her position; she is determined, and seizes her opportunity, "Carpe diem!" Esther simply gets it! Rather quickly, Esther goes from taking orders to giving orders. Esther gains the respect of her cousin, and even her husband, which is no small feat!

This is the part of Esther's transformation which relates to us most: If Esther doesn't *put her feet in the water* (i.e. Joshua 3:15); she will miss her opportunity to be used by God to save His people! Was it scary? Absolutely! But by stepping out in faith and hope, Esther becomes the savior of the Jews, for which she is still remembered to this very day! Esther goes from winning a beauty contest, and the ear of the king—to winning the hearts of her people. Esther is also a perpetual inspiration to all readers of Scripture to this day!

Transformation: Things Hoped For!

16. Do you long to experience this type of transformation? Do you long to be bold for the Lord? Are you fearful, afraid to step out into uncharted territories? Is the Lord presenting you with an opportunity right now that seems a bit risky?

   a. Sometimes we just need to give up the debate, and make it really simple, and just decide! What direction does Proverbs 3:6 give you?

   b. What did Jesus say about fear while following Him? Matthew 8:24-26:

   c. What promise can you stand on? 1 Thessalonians 5:24

✝ The Feast of Purim is instituted and the Jews have their mourning turned into a joyous holiday! Christians can celebrate Purim too, both traditionally and personally! Consider the deliverances, or the interventions, by the Lord in your life: do you remember when the Lord intervened and delivered you out of it all?

17. Record your own Purim tribute here! This can be a literal deliverance, or just a time when you knew the Lord intervened on your behalf in a significant way! Give God the glory which He is so worthy:

> "Those who do not remember the past are condemned to relive it."
> George Santayana

The celebration begins with rest and remembrance, and there is feasting and rejoicing. This attitude of rejoicing creates the natural desire for benevolence by the Jews as they care for one another, sharing in their material blessings of food and gift giving to the poor.

18. Gratitude is an attitude which produces a spirit of generosity. Record what these verses say about the poor and our particular responsibilities:

- Leviticus 25:35

- Proverbs 19:17

- Luke 3:11

- James 1:27

19. Why is it important for the Jews to celebrate Purim? See verse 28:

20. What is the nature of the letter, from verse 30?

21. What specifically are the Jews to do during Purim, from verse 31?

The Jews initiate the feast, but the Queen and Mordecai send an official letter to confirm that Purim is to be a custom celebrated, and never forgotten! There should be *fasting and lamentations . . .*

CHAPTER TEN

Read chapter ten now . . .

The extremely dramatic deliverance story of the Jews can end on any note, but the writer chooses to conclude this amazing story with one more kudo to Mordecai! Do you recall when Mordecai was overlooked for his valor when he intervenes and stops the assassination attempt on Ahasuerus? Mordecai is rewarded with the concluding distinction of honor in this story! Esther is the one, who wins the king's ear, but Mordecai is the one who tells her what she ought to do about that, and God remembers! *For Mordecai the Jew was second only to King Ahasuerus and great among the Jews.*

1. What is your most inspiring "end note," from the story of Esther?

2. What is your favorite memory verse, or any other verse, from this Bible study?

3. What is the most important message that you sense the Lord is speaking to *you* through this study?

Turning Point Prayer

God is leading you to victory! That's the good news—but it also may be the hard news. When God is having His way with you, it often seems everything is hard, including prayer! *God Unseen* certainly is having His way with the characters in the story of Esther. But it is through their hard circumstances that God is doing something truly remarkable in their lives, and the results are victorious! God leads from victory, in victory, to victory!

This can be *your* turning point prayer! Do you find yourself praying this way often, "Lord, help me . . . show me . . . ?" Sometimes praying this way is skirting personal responsibility. Sometimes we ask the Lord to do things for us that only we can do—decision making! The "help me" or "show me" pleas can simply amount to not being willing to decide to step out in obedience, honor, courage, or commitment. The Lord will help us—but He gives us free will to decide; and so we must decide first. The next time you hear those words slip out of your mouth, stop and think! Are you really asking for help with your decision—or, are you asking the Lord to decide for you on a matter which He already spoke to you about? Yes, the Lord may be having His way with you presently—but He leads you from victory, in victory, to victory! Now is a good time to settle the matter. Record your prayer thoughts . . .

This can be *your* turning point prayer! Perhaps you are doing each lesson faithfully, and now that you are at completion, you still have some *things hoped for*. Maybe you feel a bit left-out? You long for transformation. Maybe you feel as though some things just belong to other Christians, but not for you? Transformation can happen in an instant—or it can take a lifetime! Start with the verses below, today. They are only two truths from thousands. Practice what they say, and turn them into the cry of your heart!

- This is your hope! *"For nothing will be impossible with God."* Luke 1:37

- This is how! *"But we all, with unveiled face, beholding as in a mirror the glory of the Lord, are being transformed into the same image from glory to glory, just as from the Lord, the Spirit."* 2 Corinthians 3:18

Hold on, even to *the last half hour!*

Notes

More about the author . . .

Christi is a Bible study curriculum writer and the Founder and Director of WSBS, Women's Summer Bible Study. She is passionate about the Word of God, prayer, spiritual revival for the Church, and the special ministry of encouraging women in godly marriage.

Christi began women's ministry over twenty years ago in her home church, Harvest Christian Fellowship in Riverside, California. She was a women's Bible teacher in her home church, and served on Leader's Council for many years assisting with training women in spiritual leadership roles.

Christi and her husband, Larry, have been married for 35 years and live in Southern California. Christi is a homemaker and considers that her primary ministry. She is also a Bible teacher and Christian women's event speaker.

For more information about Christi or to contact her please visit her website at:
www.christirobillard.com

All of Christi's books are available on amazon.com

Made in the USA
San Bernardino, CA
29 April 2015